Workbook Seven
Of the Business Essentials
Series

SYSTEMISING YOUR BUSINESS
FOR CONSISTENT EXCELENCE

John Millar

ISBN:1536899038
ISBN-13:9781536899030

DEDICATION

I dedicate this book to my mother and father, who raised me while self-employed. They taught me to work hard and listen to everyone but to make my own choices as to what is right and what is wrong.. and oh, did I mention work hard?

Anyone who tells you to work smart not hard hasn't ever done it tough and realized that if you work smart AND hard you will achieve more than you can possibly dream.

CONTENTS

To Your Success!

PRODUCT DESCRIPTION

What keeps a huge multi-national business like McDonald's ticking over every day when they have to rely on the input of inexperienced teenagers? Systems! What keeps franchises ticking over? Systems! How do countries continue to operate with changes of government? Systems!

If your systems are obsolete, non-existent, ineffective then you can't expect your output and productivity to be any different. You will always be running around extinguishing spot fires or raging infernos because your systems don't allow for the objectification of tasks and outcomes.

This vital DVD shows you:

- The importance of systems
- How to develop systems that are appropriate and specific to your business
- How to up-skill staff in the use of systems
- How to objectify tasks so that processes and problems can be handled by anyone who is system-aware
- How to improve work quality and consistency
- The savings that can be had with introducing and training new staff
- What to do with the extra time you will save by implementing systems
- Hot to enable and empower staff to become competent and reliable decision-makers and stakeholders

Being open to the introduction of systems and embracing, rather than rejecting, them is a huge step forward for many businesses. Your business deserves to benefit from this manageable strategy.

Regards,

John Millar

Do you drive your business or does the business drive you?

Drive your systems and your systems will drive your business.

....

....

....

....

What do we actually need a system for?

We need systems to ensure what our business is going to look like when it's finished. Otherwise we will never be able to ensure whether it will actually achieve a certain sale price, that it is going to achieve particular levels of revenue at a particular profit level. We need systems to know your vision is being achieved and that you are running your business in the most profitable way.

....

....

....

....

Have you made sure that you have leveraged on every opportunity within your business?

....

....

....

System is an acronym that stands for

Saving
Your
Self
Time
Energy
Money

It's all about systemizing the routine and humanizing the exceptions.

....
....
....
....
....

Systemize your business like a corporate but humanize it like a small business.

The whole idea of leverage and systems is to make sure that you work once and get paid forever.

....
....
....
....
....

Where can you achieve this within your business?

1. ....
2. ....
3. ....
4. ....
5. ....
6. ....
7. ....
8. ....
9. ....
10 ....

> **What are some of the tasks that you can document and systemize once so you don't have to worry about them anymore and anyone can be easily trained to do them?**

1. ....
2. ....
3. ....
4. ....
5. ....
6. ....
7. ....
8. ....
9. ....
10 ....

> **The only way that you can do this is to write it down and write it all down clearly otherwise, you'll be destined for someone else to come back and ask you the same question.**

....
....
....
....

I see it time and time again in businesses where the same question is asked by different people because they haven't written it down; they haven't created a system, a process. They haven't got clear documentation so that people know what they have to do or how to do it. What a monumental waste of time!

....
....
....

If you got hit by a bus today, how would your business operate?

If it's sitting in your head, it could get lost, it could get muddy, and it could get lost in translation. You can tell a number of people the same thing at different times and it all comes out differently. If it's clearly documented you won't have this issue. What are some of the things you can leverage online tools and video to clearly document a system in your business?

1.
2.
3.
4.
5.
6.
7.
8.
9.
10

Can you use a flowchart or Gantt charts

"This exercise is to help you understand the idea of processes and systems. When I tell you to…
find the sequence of numbers starting with number 1 then 2, 3, 4 and so for in consecutive
order.
I am going to give you one minute. Strive to get to the highest number you can.
Ready…begin (time for one minute)

97	21	37	9	61	14	74	26	6	94
89	49	1	53	81	34	82	46	66	18
13	57	25	17	65	90	22	70	30	58
77	33	73	45	93	38	78	2	42	86
41	69	85	29	5	98	50	62	54	10
63	7	79	39	15	76	48	12	16	96
75	47	27	59	31	100	24	36	56	68
3	43	23	19	71	4	52	40	32	60
83	11	91	35	87	72	28	80	8	84
55	95	51	99	67	20	88	44	92	64

Now we are going to run this exercise again. But this time we are going to make use of a "system."

"Make a vertical line from top to bottom between the numbers 61 and 14."

"Next make a horizontal line from side to side between the numbers 41 and 63."

"Let's do the exercise again. BUT now search for the numbers starting in the top left quadrant. You should find the number 1. Next go the right; the top right quadrant and you will find the number 2. Next go to the bottom left to find number 3...the to the bottom right to find number 4. And continue this cycle to find the highest number"

Run the exercise again allowing one minute.

97	21	37	9	61	14	74	26	6	94
89	49	1	53	81	34	82	46	66	18
13	57	25	17	65	90	22	70	30	58
77	33	73	45	93	38	78	2	42	86
41	69	85	29	5	98	50	62	54	10
63	7	79	39	15	76	48	12	16	96
75	47	27	59	31	100	24	36	56	68
3	43	23	19	71	4	52	40	32	60
83	11	91	35	87	72	28	80	8	84
55	95	51	99	67	20	88	44	92	64

Did you notice that if you followed the system you've got far, far further because you're only looking for one number in each quadrant? You weren't searching the entire page. That's a simple example of a system and one that you can use time and time again.

So what are the basics behind the system?

There are three basic areas behind a system: the Rules, the Method and the Tools

....

....

....

....

The Rules or policy.

This is what the company is committed to. It also states what the company's position is, any particular conditions or constraints that they have and must be clear, unambiguous and not open to interpretation.

What are some examples of hard rules (what I call red rules) in your business?

1. ....
2. ....
3. ....
4. ....
5. ....
6. ....
7. ....
8. ....
9. ....
10 ....

What are some examples of hard rules (what I call red rules) in your business?

1. ....
2. ....
3. ....
4. ....
5. ....
6. ....
7. ....
8. ....
9. ....
10 ....

The Method or process and procedure.

A process is basically a set of logical, related tasks performed to achieve a defined a outcome. It sets out how the company will translate the rules or policies into action. It is also known as a procedure which follows detailed instructions to ensure that the process can be repeated with the same outcome every time even by different people.

....

....

....

....

If you got hit by a bus after you have everything systemized would your business now be able to operate without you?

What are some of the tools that you can use?
1. Forms
2. Templates
3. Standard documents
4. Notices
5. Guides
6. Checklists et cetera

Just make sure all of the tools support the process and procedure and ultimately the policy.

....

....

....

....

....

> **What level of compliance is needed in your business and how carefully must that process be completed?**

For example, this is where we talk about how things are important or less important. If the process is to actually pick your kids up from school and they finished school at three o'clock and you are five to 10 minutes late is this acceptable or unacceptable? It probably not good but it's probably not going to be the end of the world.

However, if I'm actually conducting brain surgery, is only being within a centimeter or two of the actual target area okay? I would suggest probably not!

What is ok to be close but doesn't have to be spot on inside your business?

1. ....

2. ....

3. ....

4. ....

5. ....

6. ....

7. ....

8. ....

9. ....

10 ....

What is not just ok to be close and must absolutely be spot on inside your business?

1. ....
2. ....
3. ....
4. ....
5. ....
6. ....
7. ....
8. ....
9. ....
10 ....

The cost of inefficiency inside your business directly affects your profits. You'll find that it increases your expenses, it reduces your capacity to be able to act and operate really effectively, and it does not allow you to protect your profits the way you should.

What is the cost of inefficiencies inside your business?

What is that 99% actually doing to hit your bottom-line?

What can you do to better?

1. ....
2. ....
3. ....
4. ....
5. ....
6. ....
7. ....
8. ....
9. ....

What happens to your business if you increase 99% to 99.1%, 99.2% or 99.9%?

How are we going to actually map the process?

Every process has a very distinct start and end point.

Every process consists of a series of steps that must be performed in sequence.

Remember, a process can include other processes so they can be interdependent upon each other.

As an example. There's no use of me having a manufacturing plant with fantastic process there if my stock control that allows me to produce and manufacture those goods does not the systems which allows me to have consistency of quality stock to actually manufacture.

Likewise, it's no good if I can't get it picked, packed and shipped and dispatched out the other end.

Then it's no good, again, if the process is if we're not invoicing it correctly following the accounts up and getting paid.

You can see there's a whole host of different processes which can be interrelated or interdependent upon each other and then may be able to be linked together.

The Basic Principles

- Every process has a distinct starting point and ending point.
- Every process consists of steps that must be performed in sequence.
- A process can allow for alternative actions based on decisions.
- A process can include other processes.
- A process is performed by one or more people (think 'machines')
- A process can link to other separate processes.
- A process has a means of identifying that its outcome has been achieved satisfactorily.

How can we represent these principles so that other people can actually understand them?

....

....

....

....

Symbols have been used since ancient Egyptian times to be able to show some of those things. And oftentimes, when you look at things like flowcharts as you can see in some of these say Microsoft Excel that will use consistent symbols to be able to show a termination, a process or step, a decision, a predefined process, a document, a connector, or something that interrelates to it.

Standard Symbols

| Terminate | Decision | Pre-Defined Process |
| Process (Step) | Document | Connector |

Here's a really simple example

1. Offer a drink → 2. Tea or Coffee?

Coffee → 3. Make a cup of coffee

Tea → 4. Make a cup of tea

1. So you want an ice-cream → 2. Would you like chocolate? — *No* → 4. Would you like strawberry? — *No* → 5. Here's your Vanilla ice-cream

2. Would you like chocolate? ↓ 3. Here's your chocolate ice-cream

4. Would you like strawberry? ↓ 5. Here's your Strawberry ice-cream

I'd like you to take two minutes now and actually sit down and work out how would you go about making a cup of coffee? Use those different symbols that we showed before in how to terminate the step or process and decision and then write a concise summary on the process of each step.

Create your own flow chat

Did you really understand your flowchart or could you understand somebody else's?

Did you make it over complicated? Keep it simple, stupid.

Select a process that's not too complex, something that you're familiar with and something that you would normally perform.

Are there alternative parts and decisions that can be made within that process that's within your business?

Was there more than one person involved in that process?

Is there a clear outcome or a criteria for success that you've applied for that?

And is there a really clear sequence to make sure that it all flows and how can that be linked or included within that process?

> Make sure you write down a concise summary of each step within that process and what you've learned from it.

Have you identified areas of what was missing in your process?

Remember 94% of all failures within the business are system-related. Only 6% are people related
and that most of those people-related issues I believe are let down because their process and their system were not clear.

What areas can you actually systemize inside your business? You can cover things like your marketing, accounts, administration, HR, consulting, production, delivery, trade services, operations, sales, professional services, and the list goes on.

Systems need to be not simply well-balanced but interrelated and interconnected with other clear systems which allow them to support each other.

Do you have a system that is KPI-driven?

Key performance indicator-driven systems cover everything from the owner of the business, the manager of the business and those individual areas of marketing, sales, production, administration and accounts, human resources and so on. All you MUST have these things systemized and clearly documented.

....

....

....

....

What you can actually do to improve your client fulfilment, the satisfaction level for your client, generate referrals, deliver consistently?

1. ....
2. ....
3. ....
4. ....
5. ....
6. ....
7. ....
8. ....
9. ....
10 ....

What you're doing within your lead generation and your management of the business, your functional areas of your USP and guarantee?

1. ....
2. ....
3. ....
4. ....
5. ....
6. ....

7. ....

8. ....

9. ....

10 ....

Is there a conversion process?

Is there a client fulfilment process?

Is there a business management process?

What are some of the processes that you can systemize in your business to help you today?

1. ....

2. ....

3. ....

4. ....

5. ....

6. ....

7. ....

8. ....

9. ....

10 ....

I believe that there needs to be a set of key performance indicators or KPIs for each and every position within the business, for each and every chain within the business. Do you have clearly documented position descriptions, position contracts, KPIs, budgets and required outcomes for every single position?

Have you listed each and every routine task?

Have you classified all those KPIs, all those things with how often they actually need to be done, whether it's daily, weekly, monthly, quarterly?

What are the tasks that you want to get rid of that if you systemize, documented and made clear that you'd be able to shed from out of your time so that you can be more valuable on your business?

1. ....
2. ....
3. ....
4. ....
5. ....
6. ....
7. ....
8. ....
9. ....
10 ....

An hour working on your business is usually worth 10 in your business

What are we doing now that's working great?

1. ....
2. ....
3. ....
4. ....
5. ....
6. ....
7. ....
8. ....
9. ....
10 ....

What are the things that we're doing now that could be a little bit better or could be improved upon?

1. ....
2. ....
3. ....
4. ....
5. ....
6. ....
7. ....
8. ....
9. ....
10 ....

What are we not doing but we really should be doing?

1. ....
2. ....
3. ....
4. ....
5. ....
6. ....
7. ....
8. ....
9. ....
10 ....

What are things that we are doing that perhaps we shouldn't?

1. ....
2. ....
3. ....
4. ....
5. ....
6. ....
7. ....
8. ....
9. ....
10 ....

I challenge you to do these things and when you do,
you will save more time and you will make more profit.!

John Millar

Business Essentials Series...

Disc 1 in the Business Essentials Series
Gaining Focus in Your Business
*This is about your fundamental learning skills and what you will need to do to change them to vastly improve the way you look
at your development to become a truly effective business owner not just simply remain self-employed.*

You will also give you some excellent tools to set goals, work on your plans and create a diary that will allow you to steal your time back to begin moving your business from chaos to control.

Disc 2 in the Business Essentials Series
Getting Your Financials Right
You will learn the importance of understanding your financials.

After all being in business is about making profit and having cash flow work for YOU since you are responsible for your profits.
Become your accountant and book keepers best friend by understanding more about how the financials in your business works so you can ask them better questions to maximise your profits not simply ensure tax compliance.

Disc 3 in the Business Essentials Series
Leveraging Your Business Harder
You will learn the principles of what and how to leverage far more in your business to get more from less and to work far smarter and not just harder.

Here is where you will receive some of the tools you will need to better understand how to get your business flying, what it is you need to test and measure, how to do it and WHY it's so important.

Disc 4 in the Business Essentials Series
How to Generate More Clients Profitably
This is where you will determine your uniqueness, develop a meaningful guarantee and learn the basics of good advertising.

You will gain a better appreciation between the difference of Marketing and Advertising, learn how to get the most for the least investment and ensure that you do it all profitably.

Disc 5 in the Business Essentials Series
Maximising Your Conversion Rates
Get to know how your Sales Pipeline REALLY works and how to identify who your suspects really are, convert prospects into regular shoppers and understand how much more work you can do to maximise your sales experience.

Disc 6 in the Business Essentials Series

Meet and Exceed Your Clients Expectations

Now you have new customers, how do you make sure you KEEP them, how do you wanting to come back time and again while telling their friends? ...this is where you really make a difference.

Disc 7 in the Business Essentials Series

Systemising Your Business For Consistent Excellence

Do you recognise the importance of having systems in your business and how they can improve your profitability?

We show you how to systemise like a corporate while retaining the culture of a smaller business. Understanding how we systemise for routine and humanise for the exceptions will enable you to be the best in your field every time.

Disc 8 in the Business Essentials Series

Do You Have a Champion Team with a Champion Leader?

This is about having the right people on the bus. It starts with you however so you'll learn how to maximise your own skills and then you will attract and retain the right people.

When you understand how the TEAM is the most important part of your business and what needs to be done to achieve the very best from yourselves and others you are well on your way to becoming a better manager of this invaluable resource.

Disc 9 in the Business Essentials Series

The Essentials of Getting Your Time Back.

This is where you get to redefine your time management You will understand better how you can start working far more on the business than in the business than ever before.

You will also finally find out why others can seem to fit more into their day while having a great LIFE – WORK balance (notice the order!)..

Disc 10 in the Business Essentials Series

Simply Brilliant Customer Service.

It's so easy to give mediocre or good customer service but it's just as easy to give amazing service to your customers and delight them.

You will understand the simple easy steps that you must take to provide consistently brilliant service and how to get your team excited about doing it.

Disc 11 in the Business Essentials Series

Discovering DISC and EQ not just IQ.

We believe for things to change first you must change so here you will learn why you behave as you do and just as importantly understand why other people react and act the way they do.

You will also learn what DISC really is and what it isn't. You will learn how to apply these important principles in your recruitment and team management / development.

You will learn how to use these ideas in creating a more dynamic team and discover the what and why of emotional intelligence. You will also develop key strategies for using the knowledge here and the tools we have available on our website and why we place such a massive emphasis on DISC and other tools that support, train and develop your team.

You will also learn how to use these skills and observations at home and socially not just at the workplace.

Disc 12 in the Business Essentials Series
Quality Recruitment.
Recruitment of the right people for the right reasons in the right roles for your team is so incredibly important yet so often ignored or pushed to the rear.

You will learn who the right person is for your business and the role you want filled.
You will be able to identify the right people early in the process to save yourself and them the time and money wasted with antique recruitment methodologies that just don't work anymore.

How to get the best out of your recruitment activities so you can keep the assets you acquire for the long term and get the best return from your investment.

ABOUT THE AUTHOR

John Millar is the Managing Director, Senior Business Coach Trainer and Consultant with More Profit Less Time Pty Ltd and CEO-ONDEMAND. Along with his many other business interests, John is proud to have been an associate of the most successful coaching team in the world.

He is recognized as a global leader and has been benchmarked against over 1,300 colleagues in 31 countries. John has over 25 years of hands-on ownership, management, coaching, and entrepreneurial experience in a broad range of industry sectors, including retail, wholesale, import, export, IT, trades and trade services, automotive, primary production, food services, transport, manufacturing, mining, professional services, the fitness industry, and more.

He has extensive experience developing and providing training for small to medium-sized companies and a variety of publicly listed corporate companies. John is an accomplished and talented public and professional speaker. He has been a mentor working with sales/management activities for businesses with a turnover under $100,000 per annum, over $100 million turnover, and everything in between, with great success.

John currently works with business owners and their teams across Australia and has a "Whatever it takes" attitude that has enabled him to help his clients grow their business profits by up to 800%.

If you are ready to be coached by one of the best in the business, register at:

www.ceo-ondemand.com.au

Make sure to visit www.moreprofitlesstime.com for the new online Management Development Program: The Business Essentials Series.

ACCLAIM FOR JOHN MILLAR'S
Business Coaching and Training in their own words...

"Without John Millar as my Business Coach I wouldn't have a business today."—Grant Jennings Managing Director, Jigsaw Projects

"Taking the decision to be coached and trained by John Millar was carefully considered after experiencing those who over promised and under delivered. I am pleased to say the content of his courses are the tools we all need to master as business owners. His delivery is engaging, thought provoking and empowering and after every session l came away re-energised. John always makes himself available for business building advice both via Skype and face to face beyond the scope of delivery. With his extensive personal experience in building small businesses, he knows and understands what it takes to establish and grow a business. I have no hesitation endorsing John Millar as an educator and business coach and the bonus is he is a very nice person."—Anne Lederman Managing Director FB Salons"

Johns training with my management team was excellent, it was very different from the business coaching and support I have had in the past. John was clear, thoughtful and he addressed the issues we needed to cover without us even knowing they were being addressed! His follow up has been fantastic and exactly what I needed. I would recommend John and his team to anyone looking at getting some business coaching and training done" —Wendy Crawford, Peopleworx

"In my dealings with John as our business coach, I have found him to be a motivated and insightful agent of positive change. He is able to burrow down to the root cause of issues and introduce effective forms of measurement. John then identifies and implements practical solutions and is there to provide the gentle persuasion required to ensure that results are achieved." —Mark Felton, Lindale Insurances

"You have coached and trained us so well throughout the year that we are now used to & find it easy to prepare a 90 day plan, then breaks it down to actionable bite size pieces. Planning in business & personal life certainly is important. It allows us to identify the important things & the bigger picture. Thank you for your support & guidance throughout the year. And not to mention your insight, external perspective to review & assist our business moving forward." —Linda Turner, Director Roy A McDonald Certified Practicing Accountants

"If you want to achieve sales results you never thought were possible and give yourself a competitive edge my strong suggestion is to engage John services and listen closely to what John has to say, during the time I was trained by John I was one of eight sales consultants in a national business for 10 out of the 13 months I lead the sales tally and in 1 quarter I generated three times the revenue of the national sales force combined. Johns training and experience was well worth the investment and paid big dividends. Thanks John." —Julian Fadini, Bellvue Capital

"John is a very enthusiastic trainer and business coach, he is very passionate about getting business owners and their team where they need to be. He goes the extra mile to keep ahead of the latest developments which he then uses to benefit his clients." —Darren Reddy CPA

"I have been to a few seminars and heard John speak numerous times about sales, marketing and business. He is a very knowledgeable and extremely enthusiastic business coach in all his interactions and I would recommend him to all business owners who need a sales and marketing boost!" —Andrew Heath, Managing Director, Fresh Living Group

"I worked with John Millar and found his business knowledge, passion and innovation to be inspiring. He has always been able to set (and achieve) strategic long and short-term goals both for himself and his clients without losing that personal connection he builds with everyone he meets. He has been and I believe will continue to be a strong mentor and trainer for anyone wanting to take that next step in their business." —Bree Webster, Online Marketing Guru

"Massive Action Day" – what an understatement, John Millars 4 hour frenzy challenged me to seriously review areas of my business I would not have gone to .... In this way, the process identified incongruence's in my mind, my business and my modus operandi. It's created a paradigm shift. Thanks John, the road map just got a whole lot clearer. Your friendship and insights since 2003 have been a gift to my business and I." —Andrew Reay, Counsellor, Hypnotherapist and Counsellor, Thinkshift Transformations

"John Millar is not your usual Business coach or trainer; he gets involved with you and your business and provides hands on help to make sure you follow through on his advice. He is highly motivated to help his clients and his personal guarantee certainly shows this. He has now transposed his thoughts, advice and love of good business onto a series of DVD's in his business venture – More Profit Less Time. This has excellent tips and advice for anyone either starting out or already in business. I highly recommend John to any business owner who wants to run a business and not a j.o.b.!" —Darren Cassidy, Managing Director HR2U

"I and many of my Business Partners and colleagues have worked with John since 2010 as our business oath, trainer and motivator and found him to be an extremely motivational person to assist us achieve our business goals. This company and its products allows for John's skill set to be accessed by a wider number of potential clients. His very professional DVD series is extremely good value for money and is easily accessible for all of us who are time poor. If you are looking to maximise your and your business's results and to start achieving your goals and dreams, contact John; you won't look back!!" —Mark Cleland, Mortgage Choice

"John develops real relationships with the people he comes into contact with. He is pasionate about what he does. His DVD and group training series, is full of good ideas and process to make your business better. Knowing what to do and actually doing it are two different things. John is excellent at helping you get things done." —Carey Rudd, Sales Director, Online Knowledge

"I have known John since 2004 and found him to be extremely knowledgably in both Sales and Business systems as a business coach without peer. John has provided me with business advice as well as personal coaching over the years, helping me with the running of my organisation. I'm impressed with John's DVD series where he has condensed a lot of the information in an easy to follow format that any business owner can use immediately. I wish he had released these DVDs earlier, as they are a goldmine of information, and practical how to that allow anyone to increase the profit in their business and get back valuable wasted time." —Steve Psaradellis, Managing Director, TEBA

"John's DVD and workbook delivery of his no-nonsense advice provides a low-cost option for those business owners looking to set and achieve goals that will increase profit. I found the conversational style of the DVD's easy to follow, whilst the requirement to pause the DVD and write down some action points ensured a level of commitment to the advice being provided." — Mark Felton, Lindale Insurances

"I only met John briefly at a BNI meeting and knew instantly i need to hire him for my business as my business coach. His attitude towards work and how to improve my cash line had an instant effect on before, even before I finally hired him on an official basis. I found myself thinking "what would John do" and this was only after just meeting him. I cannot see my business expend and give me "More Profit Less Time" without John's expert direction and training. If you want to succeed in business life, you need John Millar, without him you're just kidding yourself " —Leslie Cachia, Managing Director, Letac Drafting

"I can highly recommend John Millar to any business owner who wants to grow his business. When I hear very positive feedback from colleagues who are skeptics by nature about John's ability and skills, I know John will help all those he comes in contact with. John comes with a selfless nature and the willingness to work inside a client's business to make it succeed. Rare indeed!" —Darren Cassidy, Managing Director, HR2U"I first met John Millar in mid-2010 and have always found him to be of an honest and generous character that engenders an easy association with him. I love how easy he is to listen to and how passionate he is about his work and topics. John demonstrates a love for life and his work and I have no hesitation in recommending his services." —Kathie M Thomas, Managing Director, VA

"I have listened to John speak on a number of occasions and find him a very knowledgeable speaker with a passion for what he does. I have also interacted with a number of his clients and they all tell me that he helps them achieve results in their business. If you are looking for business help John is a person you can trust." —Carey Rudd, Sales Director, Online Knowledge

"John knows his stuff, he knows how the get results, John has so many great ideas in building a business and helping business owners work less and make more money. John has released a DVD set on doing just that. I have watched the 1st one and it was great, very informative and easy to understand, I happily recommend John to anyone in need of help and guidance" —Frank Eramo, Proprietor, Dynotune

"I have known John only for a short time, however the impact that he has had on me, not just my business has helped me to visualise opportunities that I began to doubt my ability to realise. He is encouraging and at the same time challenging so that he can/you can, begin to see how to maximise the business potential, John calls it being an unreasonable friend, I call it being a mate. If you have any questions about the direction of your business, if you want to seem your bottom line improve not just turnover but real profit, if you want a person who will work with you then I strongly recommend that you engage him at your earliest convenience. John is the best thing that has happened to my business. I could tell you about the way he is on track to make 1/2 a million for me on his contacts alone, but that actually sells him short, he has become like my partner in business, and cares about my success as if it was his own, we will flourish because I took the step to employ his training to help me grow. If you get a chance to get him training you, don't wait like I did, get in as quickly as possible, his time is your business and if like me your business is to make money, then every day you don't have him on retainer you lose money." —Russell Summers, Managing Director, The Give Life Centre

"It's usually easy to be mediocre in business but it's impossible when you have John Millar training you. He has been my right hand since 2003!" —David Manser, CFO, Hydrosteer

"I now have a commercial, profitable business and now it's my choice when I work IN my business and when I work ON it and have had john helping me in business since 1988. I can't imagine not having John as a part of our business." —David Wall, Director, D&K Transport

"The work John has done since 2008 coaching and training our marketing team, administration and finance teams, buyers, store managers and staff nationally have been fantastic." —Ross Sudano, Director, Anaconda Adventure Stores

"John is a creative, professional, practical and committed business coach and trainer. His approach since we first met him in 1994 to working with a client team through the application of useful tools, information and anecdotes along with his easy going & easy to understand delivery sets him apart from other business coaches that I have used in the past." —Anthony Beasley, Director, The Astra Group

"I have worked with John Millar for the since 2004 and I didn't think it was possible to achieve what we have achieved together. His business coaching, training and services just get better and better!" —Terrance Chong, Managing Director, Echo Graphics and Printing

"John's business coaching, training and support has transformed our business across Australia and New Zealand since 2008."—Rose Vis, Managing Director, VIP Australia

"We first met John in 2005, he is AMAZING at sales, marketing, operations, logistics, finance training and so much more. Since engaging John as our business coach our business has exploded, our team are happy, our clients are raving about us and my husband and I now take at least 12 weeks holidays a year, EVERY year." —Shirley Du, Director, Goldline Technology

"It's the no nonsense results driven business coaching and training focus John bought to the table that had such a massive effect on our business." —David Runkel, Director, Tracomp Fabrication and Steel

"We started working with John in early 2010, within 90 days of working with and being trained by John Millar we had the biggest and most profitable month in our 15 year history. That's impressive." —Hugh Gilchrist, Managing Director, Australian Moulding Company

"If you don't have John as your business trainer you aren't meeting your business potential." — Don Robertson, Director, Medallion Electrical Services

Thank You

www.ingramcontent.com/pod-product-compliance
Lightning Source LLC
Chambersburg PA
CBHW050410180526
45159CB00005B/2220